Kinross-shire
Then & Now

By David Millar

This bacon factory, also featured on page 18, was a long-standing operation in Milnathort.

Text © David Millar, 2020.
First published in the United Kingdom, 2020,
by Stenlake Publishing Ltd.,
54-58 Mill Square,
Catrine, Ayrshire,
KA5 6RD

Telephone: 01290 551122
www.stenlake.co.uk

ISBN 9781840338737

Printed by Blissetts,
Roslin Road,
Acton,
W3 8DH

In 1918 Glenlomond Hospital opened near Wester Balgedie as a tuberculosis sanatorium but was immediately taken over for the treatment of First World War military personnel with shell shock. However, the following year it returned to its intended use. In the late 1950s it was converted for the treatment of people with mental health disabilities and latterly part of it was used as a nursing home named Levenglen. The building on the left of the image was the original nurses' home which has now been converted into flats. A number of private houses have also been erected on the site.

Introduction

Kinross-shire lies in east central Scotland and is the second smallest county in Scotland. The area is surrounded on three sides by hills: the Ochils to the north, the Lomonds to the east, with Benarty and Cleish to the south. The greatest width from east to west is approximately 14 miles and from north to south the length is nearly 10 miles. Loch Leven, the largest lowland freshwater loch in Scotland, lies in the east of the county.

The population of the county was 6,673 in 1891 and had risen to over 13,500 in 2019. In the past most of the inhabitants were employed in agriculture, the making of cutlery, hand loom weaving and other cottage industries such as parchment and vellum making.

The building of the railways in Kinross-shire during the mid 1800s provided improvement in transport for both people and goods. At first there were two small railway companies operating the rail system: the Fife and Kinross Railway between Kinross and Ladybank and the Kinross-shire Railway between Kinross and Cowdenbeath. These lines met at Kinross (Hopefield) Station. In 1871 the Devon Valley Railway between Kinross and Alloa was completed and the introduction of this line allowed Hopefield Station to be renamed as Kinross Junction.

By 1890 the North British Railway Company had taken over the smaller companies and a new line through Glenfarg had opened. This allowed a direct rail link from Edinburgh via the Forth Rail Bridge through Kinross-shire to Perth and beyond, bringing further increased prosperity to the area. By the 1960s, however, falling passenger numbers led to the closure of these railways and by 1970 Kinross Junction had been closed to make way for the M90 motorway. Nonetheless, the construction of the Forth Road Bridge and the M90 through the county to Perth improved links with the surrounding areas and provided opportunities for increased employment. Substantial house-building also began in the county in the 1970s, a trend which has continued ever since, and while agriculture and cashmere spinning remain the major local industries, Kinross-shire has to some extent become a dormitory area with residents commuting to surrounding towns for work. Tourism also provides local employment with attractions such as golfing, fishing, curling and gliding.

Kinross-shire's main towns are Kinross and Milnathort and there are a number of hamlets and villages such as Easter and Wester Balgedie, Kinnesswood, Scotlandwell, Cleish, Carnbo and Crook of Devon. In the early 1900s a large number of picture postcards of these places were produced by local newsagents such as Andrew Gardiner and J. Christie, both of Milnathort, and David Brown of Kinross, and this book reproduces many of these with equivalent views from today. As they show, many things have changed over the decades but some sites remain the same.

Thanks are due to the people of Kinross-shire who helped in the production of this book, in particular for providing information and allowing access to photograph some of the up-to-date images.

High Street, Kinross

The north end of Kinross High Street in the 1930s, with the familiar local landmark of the Steeple in the distance. The shops on the right are largely unaltered although they have changed occupants on a number of occasions over the years. The second building on the left is the Salutation Hotel, which was originally a coaching inn dating back to around 1720 and is now one of the few remaining local pubs in Kinross.

This recent image shows that the buildings beyond the hotel have been demolished to allow vehicle access for Avenue Road and the construction of newer buildings. Recent alterations to the upper part of the High Street have resulted in a 'shared space' with the loss of most of the pavements and the introduction of bollards and other traffic calming measures.

HIGH STREET, KINROSS.

A.9042.

This view looking north from the Cross, Kinross, was taken in the 1950s and shows on the immediate left the ornate fountain which was erected in 1885 over the old Cross Well for use as the town's public water supply. On the right of the picture is the three-storey Tolbooth built around 1600. Also known as the Old County Building, this housed the county offices, court house, cells for prisoners and the keeper's accomodation. The building was restored in

1771 by Robert Adam, the famous architect who was also MP for Kinross-shire. It was eventually converted into a number of shops and dwellings and Arthur D. Emslie's grocer's shop is now occupied by Fife Computers. Apart from the introduction of modern bollards and the loss of pavements the two scenes remain remarkably similar.

The emergence of cinema-going in Kinross is evident in this image showing the Picture House sign over the entrance to the Town Hall, which was one of the various places in the town used as the cinema in the early 1930s. Other venues included church halls or meeting rooms. The first purpose-built cinema, the County, was built in Station Road in 1938 by J.B. Milne of Dundee. It had a capacity of 600 and was very popular until the appearance of television in the 1950s resulted in dwindling audiences. It was turned into a bingo hall and renamed the Rio before being demolished and the site used for housing. The Town Hall, which was built in 1841 on the site of the demolished Old Parish Church, was frequently used for meetings and dances for a good number of

years, but due to lack of use fell into disrepair and has now been incorporated into a new development of flats and houses. Just out of sight is the 80 feet-high Steeple which was built in 1761 with money raised by a specially formed Steeple Committee. The building on the extreme right was the post office for many years until it was moved further up the High Street in the 1960s. The millinery shop on the left of the earlier picture was turned into a combined fish shop and florist run by a Mr and Mrs Renton for a time, and is now a coffee shop.

High Street, Kinross, looking South.

This view of Kinross High Street looking south, when horses and carts were the main means of transport, shows the Printing Office which was run by David Brown and his subsequent family from 1866 to 1946. The business was then taken over by Alex (Zander) Farquhar for a number of years. On the

opposite side of the street is the Central Café and fish and chip shop run by the Cavellini family for many years. This business was taken over by Donato Andreucci in 1989 and is now run by his grandson, also Donato.

901

THE PIER & MUCKLE KNOWE, KINROSS

This image shows anglers setting out from the pier at Kinross on a fishing trip on Loch Leven around 1924. The loch is famous for its trout fishing and anglers come from all over the country to try their luck. In the past blue-green algae has formed on the surface of the loch from time to time but steps continue to be taken to improve the water quality and angling remains popular. The loch was also famous for curling matches (known as bonspiels) held when the loch froze over in some of the colder winters. The last Grand Match on Loch Leven was held in 1959, although there was some local curling in

the winter of 1962/63. Muckle Knowe is the small hill in the distance topped by a side entrance into the grounds of Kinross House. The pier is also now used for the ferry service to Loch Leven Castle where Mary, Queen of Scots, was imprisoned in 1567/68 and the up-to-date image shows the two blue boats at the end of the pier which are used for the ferry.

A horse sale in progress at Milnathort Auction Mart in South Street in the early 1900s. The village had two auction marts, the other being run on the opposite side of South Street by Hay & Co. The mart seen here started in 1897 and was taken over by MacDonald Fraser & Co. of Perth in 1912; it closed in 1980 and

was subsequently demolished. The site is now known as Auld Mart Business Park and contains a mixture of commercial premises and private houses and is accessed by a new route called Auld Mart Road. The Hay & Co. mart also closed in 1980; it too was demolished and houses built on the site.

Inchmerry, Milnathort.

Inchmerry was the original name for Milnathort's Church Street and the larger building and adjacent white building on the right of the earlier view was the Cockamy Farm steading. The farmhouse was on the opposite side of the road and still exists, although the farm buildings were demolished and the site taken over in the 1950s by Kay Trailers who were blacksmiths and trailer manufacturers. A new larger building was erected and formed part of their

workshop until 2011 when the premises were sold and Kay Trailers moved to Newlands Farm near Milnathort. The larger building is at present being used as a store. Out of sight on the left side of the street is the Scout and Guild Hall. Originally the building was called Inchmerry Stables. It was obtained by the Milnathort Guides and Scouts and, following renovation, was opened in 1937 and remains in use mainly by Guides and Brownies.

Cunningham's Orwell Bacon Factory (also see page 1) was erected just off Stirling Road in Milnathort by David Cunningham in 1924 and at that time employed twelve to fifteen men and girls and had a turnover of approximately 100 pigs per week. Although the factory produced pork and bacon products for shops and hotels in Perthshire, Fife and beyond, local people could also purchase meat directly from the factory. It closed in the early 1980s and was

demolished and the site has since been taken by private houses, with the access road named Mill Lade in recognition of the previous use of the Back Burn, which passes along the edge of the site and was used to provide water for the grain mill that once stood in the centre of the village.

This photograph was taken in the early 1940s, before the metal railings in front of the entrance to Milnathort Town Hall were removed for the war effort. The names of the men are not known but from left to right the uniforms indicate that they were a postman or railwayman, an Automobile Association (AA) scout (note his boots; it was common for AA men to ride motorcycles in those days), and a police constable. The modern picture shows that the Town Hall

continues to be well maintained. The building on the right, which was previously the Commercial Hotel and later the Jolly Beggars Hotel, closed some time ago and is presently under renovation.

MILNATHORT (NORTH)

D 6420

This view taken from the clock tower of Milnathort's town hall in the 1950s shows on the hill in the distance Orwell Parish Church, with the hall in front. The church was built in 1729 and the hall was added in the 1930s. Lower down, at the foot of the hill to the left, the Wellfield houses were built around 1950 for agricultural workers. Further left is the school known as the 'big' school with its open fronted shed and playground, which was built in the early

1700s and rebuilt in 1840. Primary school education in Milnathort was carried out in two buildings: the 'big' school for older children and the 'wee' school in Stirling Road for infants. Both were demolished when a new combined primary school opened in Bridgefauld Road in the late 1960s. The recent image shows that a number of houses have been built on the site of the school and on the lower right is a newly completed block of flats.

TOWN HALL, MILNATHORT.

Milnathort Town Hall with its 95 feet-high clock tower was built with funds raised by public subscription and was opened in 1855 at a cost of £800. As well as the main hall the building also contained the police station and a number of cells. In the 1940s, when this image was taken, the shop on the immediate left – now a private dwelling – was occupied by W. Duncan, butcher, and traffic bollards had been erected at the Cross to create a roundabout to control the increase in traffic at that time. The Town Hall remains in use, operated by a local committee and is a very popular venue for various meetings and functions.

This image was taken in the early 1940s in front of Stewart & Smart's garage in Stirling Road when petrol pumps were installed next to the pavement. The building in view further up Stirling Road was known as the 'wee' school and was built as a private school in 1863 by a Mr Brand, a London merchant whose wife belonged to Milnathort. The school was later bought by Mrs Reid of Thomanean, near Milnathort, who named it the Reid Memorial School after her husband. In 1914 the education authority took over the school, which was then merged with the 'big' (public) school and enabled primary

education to be under the control of the one authority. In the late 1960s a new combined primary school opened on Bridgefauld Road and the two old schools were demolished. The recent image shows that the garage, which was founded in 1926, retains the name Stewart & Smart and various alterations and additions have been carried out over the years, including a modern filling station with canopy. The garage is now under the ownership of George Shiels, who took it over a number of years ago.

OCHIL HILLS SANATORIUM MILNATHORT

Ochil Hills Sanitorium was situated about three miles north of Milnathort, 1,000 feet above sea level and surrounded by 460 acres of ground. It was built in 1902 for the treatment of tuberculosis before the introduction of antibiotics. Treatment at that time included isolation, good nutrition, fresh air and rest. The sanatorium had sixty twin-bedded rooms with various treatment rooms and resident physicians. A bus service was provided to and from Milnathort,

as most of the domestic and other staff were recruited locally. The sanatorium closed in 1986 and following two subsequent fires, in 2001 and 2003, the buildings were deemed unsafe and demolished and the site was cleared. Very little evidence of the buildings now exists and the current image is of an approximate location of the building, although it shows that the pond can still be seen through the undergrowth.

Balgedie Toll.

The old tollhouse at Balgedie stands at the junction of the Milnathort–Leslie road (A911) and the Mawcarse road (B919) and dates back to 1534 when it was used for the collection of tolls from travellers using the roads. The collection of tolls ended in the late 1800s and the building was converted into the Balgedie

Tavern as this image from around 1910 shows. Further alterations and extensions have been carried out over the years and, in recognition of its original purpose, the establishment is now called the Balgedie Toll Tavern.

Main Street, Kinnesswood

Kinnesswood, looking southeast down what is now the A911 in the early 1900s. The village shop can be seen in the distance and still exists. It is thought that in early days the villages on the eastern shore of Loch Leven may have been fishing settlements before the water level receded, probably as a result of Loch Leven being lowered in 1828. This resulted in the population being some distance from the shore. Kinnesswood was famous for the manufacture of

vellum and parchment from animal skins, which were mainly used for writing materials from the sixteenth century to the early twentieth century and were supplied from Kinneswood to the Register House in Edinburgh. The originators of this trade may have been the Priors of St Serf's Island on Loch Leven.

Michael Bruce's Cottage, Kinnesswood.

This image shows in the foreground the Kinneswood cottage on the road known as The Cobbles where Michael Bruce, a noted Scottish poet, was born in 1746. The son of a weaver, he attended the local parish school and then, showing signs of literary talent, went to Edinburgh University with the help of a legacy from a local farmer. After university he studied theology for a short time and had two spells teaching, but in 1767 he became ill and died of

consumption. Known as 'the 'Gentle Poet of Lochleven', his poems include 'Elegy written in Spring' and 'Ode to the Cuckoo'. In 1903 a trust was set up to restore the cottage and turn it into a small museum dedicated to the poet, which opened in 1906 and can still be visited today.

Kinnesswood , The Main St .

In the centre of Kinnesswood is the shop with the garage opposite. The garage was started in 1925 by Tom Buchan and is still being run by the Buchan family.

The shop was run by the Sharp family for many years but is now also being run by the Buchans. In the recent image, the telephone box is of course no longer required but is being retained and used as a book exchange, organised by the local community.

MAIN STREET LOOKING WEST, KINNESWOOD

In the eighteenth and nineteenth centuries the main occupations in Kinneswood were crofting and weaving. This view taken around 1929 shows the Lomond Hotel on the left while on the right is an example of the traditional single-storey weavers' cottages common to the area. The hotel has unfortunately

been closed for a number of years and planned development of the site was to include the retention of the part of the existing building adjacent to the Main Street. However, it has been allowed to further deteriorate and incorporation into a new development is looking less likely as time goes on.

Street Scene. Scotland Wells.

Scotlandwell in the 1930s, looking north from the junction of the Main Street and Leslie Road. The white building on the right was an eighteenth century inn called the Loch Leven Tavern; extended over the years, it is now known as the Well Country Inn. Portmoak Parish School and headmaster's house are just out of sight on the left, and in the early years pupils began and ended their education in the school. In later years, most of the older pupils were

transferred to Kinross Junior Secondary School. In 1960 a replacement primary school was built in nearby Kinneswood and this has been enlarged a number of times over the years. The house on the near right in the older image was at one time used as a toll house and was demolished in the early 1900s.

The Well, Scotlandwell

This Scotlandwell postcard from the early 1900s shows the well, which is situated down a short lane off Main Street and is reputed to produce waters with medicinal properties. The Romans first discovered these around 2,000 years ago and over the centuries they attracted many pilgrims; allegedly, Robert the Bruce used them as a cure for leprosy. Around 1860 an ornamental structure was built over the well by Thomas Bruce of Arnot, a direct descendant of Sir

William Bruce, the architect for Kinross House. The work was done as part of a village improvement scheme which included landscaping and the renovation of a number of surrounding cottages, all financed by Thomas Bruce. The recent image shows that the well and canopy have been refurbished in recent years.

Lochleven Sluices.

In 1828 one of the largest water engineering projects in Scotland at that time was started. This involved the lowering of the level of Loch Leven by four and a half feet to reclaim land for the Kinross Estate. The work included the hand digging of a straight, four-mile channel or 'cut' from the south-east corner of the loch to Auchmuirbridge and the building of these sluices near Findatie to control the flow of water, which was used as a source of power for a number

of paper and other mills in Fife. The sluices, which remain in use, were built by Robert Hutchison, a mason from Coaltown of Balgonie, using sandstone from Nivingstone Quarry in the nearby Cleish Hills. Tree growth prevents access to the viewpoint of the original photograph but the recent image shows that the sluices remain virtually unchanged.

ENTRANCE TO CROOK OF DEVON VILLAGE

Crook of Devon, looking west along what is now the A977. The corner shop has now been converted into a house but the recent image shows that there is no significant change to the houses on the north side of the street, although on the opposite side, just out of sight behind the corner shop, new houses have

been built. The original name for Crook of Devon was Fossoway (named after the parish in which it stands) and the name Crook of Devon was derived from the course of the River Devon which turns back on itself near the village.

The second stop on the Devon Valley Railway line out of Kinross was the station at Crook of Devon, which opened in 1863 and closed when passenger services ended in 1964. Very little evidence of the station's existence remains as houses have been built on the site. However, the developer has thoughtfully inserted an engraved stone with the inscription 'Devon Valley' in the wall adjacent to the site. One of the new houses has been named Station House,

Within the photo:
DEVON VALLEY

CYCLEWAY
& FOOTPATH

NO HORSES OR
MOTORISED
VEHICLES

THIS IS NOT A RIGHT OF WAY
AND SHALL BE CLOSED
1st FEBRUARY EACH YEAR

which is used as the manse for the local minister. The whole Devon Valley line took twenty years to complete between 1851 and 1871 and involved the building of two viaducts nearly 400 feet in length and the diversion of the River Devon.

The Crook of Devon Paper Mill was situated between the River Devon and the Main Street near the centre of the village. Originally known as the Lint Mill, the business was taken over by John Luke in 1827 and produced wrapping papers. The Luke family had its roots in Crook of Devon, going back generations, and there are plaques both in the local church and on the churchyard wall commemorating the service of John Luke and his son James as

church elders. The mill was taken over by Robert Livingston in 1904 and closed around 1911. It then fell into disrepair and was eventually demolished. The recent image shows an approximate view of the mill site, as the original viewpoint is inaccessible. A sign (inset) indicating 'Lukes Mill' has been erected on the wall at the entrance to the mill site.

POST OFFICE and BUNGALOW - RUMBLING BRIDGE

With the railway station and hotel close by, Rumbling Bridge's Bungalow Tearoom and the house containing the post office would have been busy with tourists when this image was taken in the early 1900s.

The tearoom has been demolished but the adjacent house, minus the post office, remains largely unaltered.

Blairingone on the A977 between Kinross and Kincardine lies at the western edge of Kinross-shire and although some of the houses have been modernised, very little has changed in the intervening 80 or so years between these two images, apart from improvements to the road surface and pavements.

The village has its origins in the middle ages when it was the site of forges that made swords and other weapons of war.

Bridgend, Kelty

The southern border between Fife and Kinross-shire is formed by the Kelty Burn which runs under this bridge at the north end of Kelty, seen here around 1912. Originally the area on the Kinross side of the bridge was known as Bridgend. Unusually, the houses, most of which were occupied by coal miners working in the Blairadam estate, are built with their gable ends facing the road.